SHANG DYNASTY CHINA

Tracey Kelly

W

FRANKLIN WATTS
LONDON•SYDNEY

First published in 2014 by Franklin Watts

Copyright © Franklin Watts 2014

Franklin Watts
338 Euston Road
London, NW1 3BH

Franklin Watts Australia
Level 17/207 Kent Street
Sydney, NSW 2000

Series editor: John C Miles
Editor: Sarah Ridley
Art director: Peter Scoulding
Series designer: John Christopher/White Design
Picture research: Kathy Lockley

Dewey number: 931

Hardback ISBN 978 1 4451 3403 1
Library eBook ISBN 9781 4451 3404 8

Printed in China

Franklin Watts is a division of Hachette Children's Books,
an Hachette UK company.

www.hachette.co.uk

CONTENTS

WHO WERE THE SHANG?

Around 3,600 years ago, during China's Bronze Age, the Shang Dynasty (about 1600–1050 BCE) ruled the lands of the North China Plain. The Shang built sophisticated cities including Yin Xu, near modern-day Anyang, their last capital. They also buried many objects in tombs, some of which have been discovered by archaeologists.

4

A bronze wine vessel dating from the early years of the Shang Dynasty, around 1600 BCE.

Amazing inventions

The Shang worshipped not only gods of nature, but also their ancestors, whom they believed could help them from beyond the grave. They made astonishing advances in writing, bronze technology, art and warfare. The invention of writing gave the Shang ability to create a government with specific jobs, and to rule and expand its lands. Metalworking technology led to the building of chariots and efficient weapons and tools, which revolutionised transport, farming and warfare.

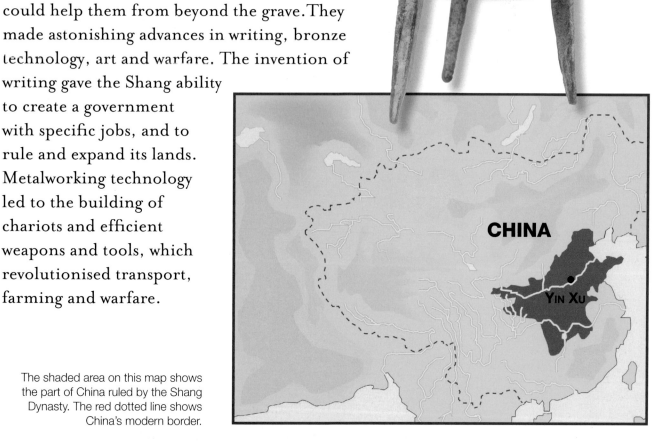

CHINA

YIN XU

The shaded area on this map shows the part of China ruled by the Shang Dynasty. The red dotted line shows China's modern border.

The archaeological remains of Yin Xu, the last capital of the Shang Dynasty, date back to 1300 BCE. The area is now a World Heritage Site and some of the ruins form part of this museum.

Lasting legacy

In 1046 BCE, the Zhou leader King Wu won the Battle of Muye against the last Shang king, Di Xin (also called King Zhou). This battle ended the Shang Dynasty. But the Zhou Dynasty (1046–256 BCE), and all the Chinese dynasties up until the last, Qing Dynasty (1644–1911), built upon the amazing achievements of the Shang. Great strides were made in the arts, literature, technology, cuisine, government and weaponry, to make China one of the strongest, most unique and enduring cultures on Earth.

 ## Dating the Shang

In the past, it has been tricky for scholars and archaeologists to accurately date the Shang Dynasty, and even today many experts disagree on dates. Recent estimates, such as those of the Xia-Shang-Zhou Chronology Project of 1996–2000, date the Shang from around 1600 BCE to 1046 BCE.

GREAT METROPOLIS

The ruins of the city of Yin Xu (near modern-day Anyang) were first discovered on the Yellow River plain in China in 1928. Its buildings and burial grounds gave archaeologists concrete evidence that the Shang Dynasty had been a real culture – not just a legend, as people had once thought.

City life

At Yin Xu, the Shang built a walled city for the royal family, priests and nobles. Its palaces and temples had wooden pillars and thatched roofs built on strong earth foundations. The city was closed off to normal people, but outside its walls were villages, markets, homes and shops, and a burial ground. Workers and farmers lived in dwellings cut into the ground, with a roof on top. Living half underground had its advantages: people were protected from bad weather.

Cutting edge

The Sanxingdui people, from south-western Sichuan Province, China, lived at the same time as the Shang. Not as much is known about their culture except that they left behind unique bronze sculptures, including heads with eerie faces covered in gold leaf. Over 40 of these were found at one site, and archaeologists think they were worshipped.

One of the life-size bronze heads created by the Sanxingdui people.

This picture shows Chinese archaeologists excavating a Shang Dynasty tomb at Anyang, dating from c. 1200 BCE.

Carbon 14

Archaeologists date Shang objects using a method called carbon dating. All living things on Earth contain an element called carbon, and when a life form dies, the amount of carbon 14 it contains lessens at a steady rate. Scientists can tell how long a person or a plant has been dead by measuring the amount of carbon 14 left in a bone or a seed, for example.

 ## Around the world

1273–1244 BCE Middle East
King Shalmanesar I builds a temple and palace at Nineveh in present-day Iraq, the oldest city in ancient Assyria.

900 BCE Greece
The city-state of Sparta is founded. After defeating Athens in the Peloponnesian War, it becomes the leading city in ancient Greece.

300–800 CE Central America
The ancient Mayan city of Tikal – located in present-day Guatemala – flourishes.

AN UNUSUAL QUEEN

Fu Hao (died c. 1200 BCE) was King Wu Ding's queen, one of his 64 wives. Her extravagant tomb, discovered in 1976, shows that she was a very important person, with many responsibilities as well as luxuries. Objects in the tomb also reveal much about how Shang society was organised.

Unusual queen

From the wealth of objects and inscriptions on oracle bones found in her tomb, we know that Fu Hao was not only a queen, but also one of the most powerful military leaders of her time. She led an army of 13,000 soldiers into battle and was involved in making peace treaties. As an adviser to the king, Fu Hao also conducted important ceremonies, some of which included human and animal sacrifices.

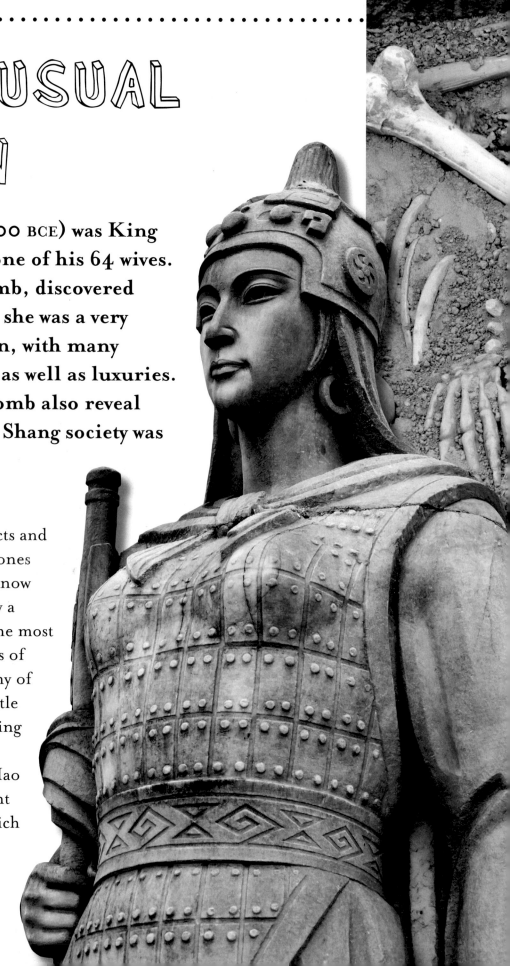

A large statue of Fu Hao guards the modern-day entrance to her tomb.

Social hierarchy

Shang society was a hierarchy with many levels of rank. The king and family were at the top, followed by the nobility. Nobles held specialised jobs in the government and the army that were passed down within families; this system carried on through later dynasties in China. Priests came next in importance then craftsmen, merchants and farmers. At the very bottom of society were the slaves, who had very few rights.

These skeletons were found in Fu Hao's tomb and date from c. 1200 BCE.

9

Cutting edge

Thousands of objects were found in Fu Hao's tomb, showing the amount of wealth and leisure time enjoyed by royalty. Over 400 items made of bronze – such as weapons, bells and tiger heads – were unearthed, as well as cowrie shells, jewellery and food vessels made of jade and pottery, and stone, ivory and bone objects. At the time of discovery, Fu Hao's burial chamber was the only Shang tomb that had not been disturbed by grave robbers.

 Around the world

c. 3050–350 BCE Egypt
Society is made up of many levels, but men and women from all classes are equal under the law, except slaves.

c. 800–1500 CE Europe
A feudal society operates, with land-owning lords, vassals, who were the tenants, and peasants who worked the land.

1603–1867 CE Asia
In Japan, a system called shinōkōshō places samurai warriors at the top and merchants at the bottom level of society.

STUNNING SCULPTURE

The motifs or designs in Shang art are lively and intricate. Animals worked into bronze and jade sculptures, or swirling patterns etched onto pottery and bone, are common. Images were also painted onto silk robes — but only fragments of these have survived the centuries.

10

Fierce face

The *taotie* is a part-animal, part-human face, with protruding, ferocious eyes and a nose in the middle. It sometimes has jaws and fangs, ears and horns, as well as legs and tails. This motif is found on many ritual vessels, but archaeologists are not sure of its meaning. The Shang were also masters of abstract design, using swirling or geometric patterns.

This bronze vessel from 13th–10th century BCE has taotie images on its legs.

Dating from 12th century BCE, this bronze wine container shows a tiger eating someone.

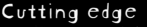

Cutting edge .

As well as artwork in bronze, the Shang worked with ivory, which comes from the tusk of an animal and was used to make jewellery and small objects. A striking carved ivory cup, inlaid with turquoise, was found in the tomb of Fu Hao. The craftsman who made it probably used the tusk of an elephant.

Tiger tales

One motif often found on vessels (containers) used in religious ceremonies is that of a tiger devouring a human, shown in the main picture. Some archaeologists think the tiger figure represents a shaman, someone who communicated with the spirits, and his helper spirit. Shang Dynasty artists were obsessed with creating animal figures, including rhinoceros, elephants, horses, birds and sheep. Some of these are realistic but they are often mysterious, imaginary creatures that combine the features of one or more animals to create mythical beasts.

11

Around the world

c. 460 BCE Greece
A grand bronze sculpture of Poseidon is created. In the 1920s, it was recovered from an ancient shipwreck located close to Cape Artemesium, Greece.

c. 800–1200 CE Pacific
Giant moai statues with mysterious faces are built by native Polynesian people on Easter Island.

c. 100 BCE Europe
Roman sculptors begin to fine-tune techniques for sculpting delicate features in marble, such as the pupil and iris of the eye.

BEAUTIFUL BELLS

The Shang were music lovers, and played a range of instruments, from beautifully decorated bells, to cymbals, wind instruments and drums. Music was played for the royal family and government officials as part of religious rituals and ceremonies.

Nao bells

12

Bronze, bell-shaped instruments called *nao* bells were made in sets of three to five bells of different sizes. Each nao bell was tuned so it could produce the sound of three notes. Together a set of bells could play all the notes in a musical composition. In southwestern China, stone chimes were found, which the Shang hung in a frame and struck to make them sound.

Cutting edge

From the Shang Dynasty onwards, China had one of the oldest forms of orchestra in the world. Players would accompany religious and royal ceremonies. No written music survives until the Zhou Dynasty, which followed the Shang, but experts have discovered a lot from studying how the instruments sound.

Dating from the 1300–1030 BCE, this bronze nao bell was found at Anyang.

Pipes, flutes and rhythm

Some of the earliest panpipes found in China date back to the Shang Dynasty. They were made from a series of hollow tubes or 'pipes' of different lengths, tied together in a row; when the player blew air across the top holes, the pipes made different notes. The flute is also an ancient instrument, and the Shang made theirs from bone. Cymbals and drums (right), also made out of bronze, were used to keep the rhythm.

Drums, such as this bronze instrument from 15th–14th century BCE, kept the beat in Shang music.

13

Around the world

2000 BCE Greece
The first lyres – U-shaped stringed instruments – are played in the Cyclades on Minoan Crete.

700 BCE Greece
People begin to study music theory, including the notes and intervals of different musical scales.

396 BCE Greece
The Olympic Games, held in the western Peloponnese, feature competitions for trumpeters. The tradition continues until 217 CE.

A BIG DING

The Shang Dynasty was part of China's Bronze Age. Bronze became a symbol of power, and only people with great wealth could afford to own luxurious objects made from this metal. Like most bronze vessels, the highly decorated ding — a type of cauldron — was made for use in ceremonies.

14

Bronze works

Because bronze is such a durable metal, intricate designs and details have remained intact for over 2,000 years. Bronze wine and food vessels were an important part of rituals for burial and ancestor worship — in fact, their sheer number tells us how much the Shang valued rituals. Finds range from small objects, such as figures and wine cups, to huge food vessels weighing up to 900 kilograms.

Simple knifes, made with stone blades, were used by Shang peasants.

Cutting edge

While bronze was used for ritual weapons, peasants and farmers used tools and weapons made from stone and wood, such as axes, sickles and hammers. Knives were also made with sharpened stone blades, and arrowheads were chiselled to a sharp point before being attached to the arrow shaft.

Casting a mould

An alloy made of copper and tin, bronze is a hard metal that must be heated into a semi-liquid form before being shaped. The Shang developed a sophisticated method for bronze-making called piece-mould casting. First, a mould was made out of clay and a design was carved into it. Then, molten bronze was poured into the mould, and when hardened, this was cracked away to reveal the bronze piece inside.

This ritual ding was made by pouring molten bronze into mould pieces, around 14th–12th century BCE.

Around the world

c. 2500 BCE Egypt
The ancient Egyptians invented a technique to create filigree – fine metal wire worked into a design – for manufacturing gold objects.

c. 2000 BCE Greece
The pottery wheel is introduced on Minoan Crete. This allows potters to easily make food and drink vessels, storage jars and figures out of clay.

2000-1500 BCE Europe
Bronze work is introduced into Britain from continental Europe, probably by the Bell Beaker people, linked to Stonehenge.

GHOSTLY CHARIOT

According to Shang inscriptions, people started using chariots around 1200 BCE. They may have seen this technology being used by people who lived in the Caucasus or Central Asia.

Hunting and war

16

Pulled by two horses, the chariot had a rectangular basket with wooden or rattan walls, in which the driver and riders stood. The basket was fixed to a draught pole and a yoke, used to attach the horses. First used by the nobility for hunting, chariots were soon used in warfare by commanders and soldiers, to conduct troops into battle and move across the battlefield.

Cutting edge

The earliest form of money in China was the cowrie shell, the shell of a sea snail. In Fu Hao's tomb, over 6,000 cowrie shells were found for her to use in the afterlife – meaning she could do a lot of shopping! When the natural supply of cowrie shells began to run out, the Shang made imitation cowrie shells out of bone, stone or bronze to use as money.

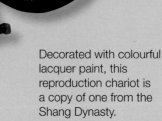

Decorated with colourful lacquer paint, this reproduction chariot is a copy of one from the Shang Dynasty.

This chariot burial with horse skeletons was found in a Shang noble's grave.

Dead end

Chariots — and their horses — were sometimes buried with royalty or military commanders. At a site in Xiaotun, 16 chariot burials have been excavated. The horses were laid out in neat rows, so that they faced eastward, the direction in which the sun rises.

 Around the world

2400 BCE Middle East
War chariots are first used by the Sumerians in Mesopotamia. They are pulled by donkeys.

1st century BCE Europe
The ancient Romans use sprung wagons for overland journeys. This helps them to travel and rule the many lands of the Roman Empire.

pre-1500s CE Africa
Manillas — copper and brass bracelets — are used as a form of money in Benin, Africa.

GEOMETRIC CUP

Food was so important to the Shang that, according to legend, Tang, the first Shang emperor, appointed renowned cook Yi Yin as his prime minister. Meals were based on grains, fruit, vegetables and fish, plus meat for those who could afford it. Pottery cups and bowls were used for daily meals, and more elaborate bronze vessels for rituals.

18 Varied flavours

While rice is a main staple of the modern Chinese diet, in Shang times, millet and wheat were widely eaten. The Shang used cooking techniques such as steaming, stir-frying and deep-frying. They flavoured dishes with sweet, hot, sour or spicy sauces, and cut food into bite-sized pieces so they could be eaten with chopsticks.

Discovered in the tomb of Fu Hao (see p. 8), this pot was used for cooking rice and dates from the period before 1200 BCE.

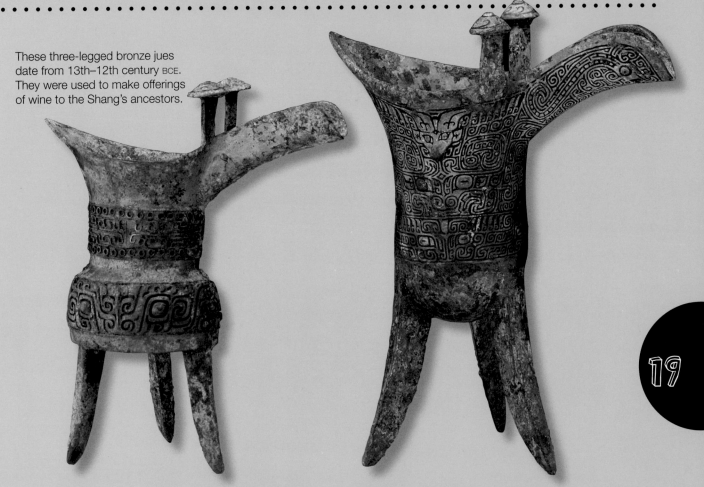

These three-legged bronze jues date from 13th–12th century BCE. They were used to make offerings of wine to the Shang's ancestors.

19

Cutting edge

The Shang held banquets to honour their ancestors as though they were alive. Many types of wine cup have been found, so we know that wine was important – not only for everyday drinking, but for religious ceremonies. A special bronze cup called a jue, with tripod legs, was used to heat a cereal wine made from millet.

Rhino stir-fry?

People ate meals made from many types of fish and a variety of meats — some of which might sound unusual today. They caught fish, clams, molluscs and shrimp, and ate chicken, wild cattle, horse, pig and deer. But sometimes, rhinoceros, elephant and tiger were on the menu as well!

 ## Around the world

3000 BCE South America
Potatoes are first grown in the Andes Mountains. They are introduced to Europeans during the 16th century.

2700 BCE Central America
Corn or maize is first grown as a crop in Mesoamerica. It later becomes the staple food for many cultures.

1500 BCE Europe/Asia
People begin to plant crops and to farm the Eurasian steppes. Later, farming spreads across the world.

GREEN BEADS

Just as people do today, the Shang enjoyed making themselves look attractive. While peasants and farmers could afford very few luxuries, the royalty and nobility wore fine jewellery and silk robes. Stunning jade pieces, such as necklaces, earrings, rings and hair combs, have been found amongst Shang settlements, as well as bone hairpins and bronze mirrors.

20

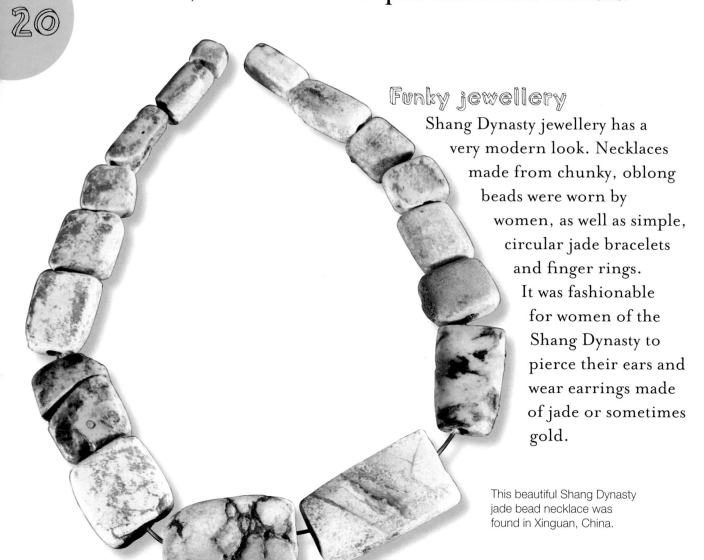

Funky jewellery

Shang Dynasty jewellery has a very modern look. Necklaces made from chunky, oblong beads were worn by women, as well as simple, circular jade bracelets and finger rings. It was fashionable for women of the Shang Dynasty to pierce their ears and wear earrings made of jade or sometimes gold.

This beautiful Shang Dynasty jade bead necklace was found in Xinguan, China.

This Shang tiger is made from jade (see below). It has a hole in its tail to allow it to be worn as a pendant.

21

Cutting edge

Jade is a hard, semi-precious stone that was highly valued by the Shang. It was used to create jewellery, cups, containers, statues and trinkets. The stone comes in many hues, from shades of green, to browns, yellows, pinks and the most prized of all – white. Owning jade jewellery was a status symbol among the Shang, just as wearing a diamond bracelet or watch is today.

Carved hairpins

Both men and women wore their long hair coiled in a bun, kept in place with a hairpin. Women's hairpins were more elaborate than men's, sometimes carved with tiny animal heads such as a phoenix. Around 500 bone hairpins were found in Fu Hao's tomb alone. The finished look was not left to chance — four mirrors made of polished bronze were also found in her tomb.

 ## Around the world

c. 2686 BCE Egypt
The ancient Egyptians wore ornate jewellery, such as pendants, hair beads, bracelets and belts.

c. 800-700 BCE Europe
Gold workers in Ireland crafted gold collars to wear as jewellery. A famous example is the Shannongrove Gorget.

c. 1300 CE Asia
Marco Polo reports that the Kayan women of Thailand use heavy neck rings as jewellery, to stretch their necks artificially.

FORTUNE TORTOISE

The Shang developed one of the oldest systems of writing in the world. They created a set of characters or ideograms to represent word ideas, which has been the basis of the Chinese written language ever since. Some of their writing survives as oracles carved onto tortoiseshell and cattle bones.

22

Cracked future

As part of the Shang religion, the king asked questions of the gods and ancestors using oracle bones to predict the outcome. For example, he might ask, "Will the queen have a healthy son?" The priest carved the question onto a bone or shell, and on the other side hollowed out a number of dips. Next, he took a heated rod and inserted it into the hollow dips. This caused cracks to appear, which the priest interpreted. He recorded the answer on the front of the oracle bone or shell.

Shang priests carved the first Chinese writing onto tortoise shells, as here, before 1122 BCE.

Cutting edge

The Shang also kept written records on strips of bamboo or silk, but these have decomposed over the centuries. Chinese people of later dynasties wrote elegant poems and painted scenes on silk and bamboo. Nobles and government officials were expected to learn how to write poetry and to paint, as well as master more practical skills.

Men of bronze

23

In the later Shang Dynasty, inscriptions were also made on bronzes. In this way, the priests recorded the history of dynasties and timelines of kings. From these records, oracle bones and artefacts, archaeologists have pieced together a lot of the puzzle about how the Shang lived.

This bronze bell shows examples of both Shang and Zhou scripts.

Around the world

2000 BCE Greece
The Minoan civilisation invents a hieroglyphic script, called Cretan script, on the island of Crete. It has not yet been deciphered.

1000–800 BCE Greece
The earliest known examples of the Greek alphabet appear.

196 BCE Egypt
The Rosetta Stone is carved using three scripts: hieroglyphs, demotic and Greek. This makes it possible to work out the meaning of all three.

MOON CALENDAR

The Shang Dynasty developed a very precise calendar system. Expert astronomers studied the movements of the Sun, Moon, planets, constellations and events such as the appearance of comets, to create accurate timekeeping. These calculations were then carved onto oracle bones.

24

Lunar lengths

Shang astronomers created a complex lunar calendar that was based on the phases of the Moon and its cycle of movement across the sky. The calendar was broken down into 12 months of 29 or 30 days. But since a solar year is 365 1/4 days long, one week was added every seven years. The calendar's accuracy was remarkable, especially since astronomers did not have telescopes or computers but worked using brain power alone.

This Shang oracle bone may have been used as a calendar to keep track of dates and times.

Cutting edge

Astronomers used a complex system of mathematics to work out the Shang calendar. They were among the first to use the decimal system, in which numbers can be broken into small parts for greater accuracy. The Shang were already using the 64 mathematical hexagrams set out in the *I Ching* (right) – an important book containing philosophy and a method of divination or fortune-telling, but the first written example of the complete *I Ching* dates from the Zhou Dynasty.

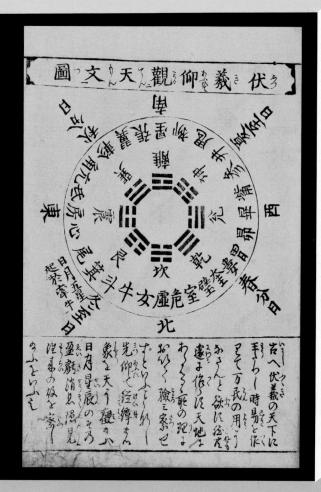

Royal watch

It was the king's personal responsibility to understand the seasons, so the calendar was important for his reputation. Being able to predict the weather was vital to know when to sow seeds and harvest crops. If grain or vegetables were sown at the wrong time and crops failed, for example, many of his people would starve and die.

Around the world

c. 450 BCE Central America
The Maya develop the Long Count Calendar, based on a ritual cycle of 260 named days and a year made up of 365 days.

450 BCE Greece
A star calendar is created by Meton and Euctemon. This tracked the movements of the stars and constellations.

928 CE Middle East
The first known astrolabe (an instrument measuring the skies) is made by Mohammad al-Fazari, an Islamic astronomer.

FEARSOME AXE

Oracle bones reveal that Shang kings constantly waged war with cities and villages outside their kingdom. But the Shang were often the victors: their military might was fierce, as their weapons gave them a huge advantage in battle.

26

Cutting edge

Di Xin (or Zhou), the last king of the Shang, ruled from 1075–1046 BCE . He was known to be cruel and corrupt – and he drank a lot! He and his queen Da Ji dug a pond big enough for canoes, and filled it with wine for parties. Showing no mercy to prisoners, Di Xin tortured people over hot coals and laughed at their screams. In 1046, Zhou commander Jiang Ziya invaded Shang lands at the Battle of Muye, and took over Di Xin's territories. The battle marked the end of the Shang Dynasty and the beginning of the Zhou Dynasty (1046–256 BCE).

A bronze halberd from the16th–11th century BCE is an example of the deadly weaponry of the Shang.

Killing fields

Bronze technology revolutionised the way the Shang fought. They developed deadly weapons, such as the bronze-tipped halberd, a cross between a spear and a battle-axe, and a bow that found its target with great accuracy. The horse-drawn chariot, probably brought in from western Asia, made it easier for warlords to command troops and made soldiers swift in battle.

With a face scary enough to frighten enemies, this bronze 'yue' axe dates from 1300–1030 BCE.

Peasants and prisoners

Most Shang soldiers were peasant farmers who were forced to leave their fields and fight for their warlords. Prisoners of war were taken from neighbouring tribes — sometimes as many as 30,000 at a time — and usually became slaves. Sometimes they were sacrificed and buried with their masters.

Around the world

23,000 BCE Europe
The oldest boomerang ever discovered is made of mammoth tusk. It was found in a cave in Poland in the 1980s.

1000 BCE Europe
In ancient Britain, swords are used for warfare and also thrown in rivers as ritual offerings to the gods.

800–1300 CE China
Gunpowder is invented, followed by simple firearms and bombs in the Song Dynasty (900–1279).

JADE TALISMAN

The Shang worshipped Shang Di, the supreme god, as well as gods who ruled nature: the Sun, Moon, wind and rain. They also worshipped their ancestors. When a person died, they were buried with a talisman, such as a decorated plaque, to bring good luck and as protection against evil spirits.

A jade *bi* disc dating from 14th–11th century BCE was used to protect its owner in the afterlife.

28

Hungry ancestors

The Shang believed in life after death, but also believed that their ancestors continued to help members of their families living on Earth. People believed that disasters would happen unless an animal was sacrificed to 'feed' hungry ancestors and keep them strong. If a person faced an especially large problem, they might even offer humans as sacrifice to ensure their ancestors would help out with a solution.

Cutting edge

Flat jade discs called *bi* were often placed on the bodies of dead people. It is thought that bi were a symbol of the sky or heaven. People believed that these lucky charms protected the deceased on their journey to the afterlife, and were used much as a cross might be placed on a present-day Roman Catholic before burial.

The Shang once offered wine to their ancestors using this exquisite ram's head bronze vessel, 13th–11th century BCE.

Funeral rites

Shang funeral rites were harsh by today's standards. Nobles were buried, not only with food and wine vessels, toiletries, chariots and animals, but with servants — and sometimes even family members, who were killed or buried alive in the tomb. If a cook prepared food for someone on Earth, it was thought he or she would carry on the same job after death, for example.

Around the world

c. 2600 BCE Middle East
Queen Puabi of Mesopotamia is buried in a stone tomb, surrounded by gold jewellery and 52 servants.

1500 BCE Greece
Gold death masks are made at Mycenae, in Greece, including the famous mask said to be of Agamemnon.

c. 1323 BCE Egypt
The 19-year-old Pharaoh Tutankhamun dies. His mummy is laid to rest in a gold sarcophagus (coffin) in the Valley of the Kings.

GLOSSARY

abstract An art design that uses patterns of shapes, textures and colours.

alloy A metal that is made from two or more other metals, to make it stronger. For example, bronze is made of two-thirds copper and one-third tin.

ancestors People in the past; forefathers.

bi A circular disc with a hole in the middle, used as a talisman to protect the dead in the afterlife.

Bronze Age A period of prehistory following the Stone Age, where civilisations discovered how to make bronze weapons and tools.

cowrie A type of sea snail. Cowrie shells were used as a form of money by the Shang.

ding A large ceremonial container made of bronze and used in ancient Chinese worship.

dynasty A line of rulers where power is passed down to other family members.

Fu Hao A Shang queen (died c. 1200 BCE) who was an important military commander and also conducted ceremonies for her husband, King Wu Ding.

halberd A weapon that combines a spear and a battle-axe.

hierarchy A system of government where groups of people are ranked above other groups according to how important they are.

jue A bronze cup with tripod legs, used to heat wine during religious rituals in ancient China.

lunar calendar A calendar that is based on the phases of the Moon and its movements across the sky.

millet A cereal grown in warm areas, with small seeds that may be cooked or ground into flour.

motif A decorative design or idea that appears often in art or sculpture.

nao bells Large, bronze musical instruments with a bell-like shape.

oracle bones Bones from cattle or another large animal (also tortoise shells), used in ancient China for divination (fortune-telling).

shaman A healer who is believed to have magic powers to cure a person of disease or tell the future.

staple A food that makes up an important part of the diet, such as bread or rice.

talisman An object that is thought to have magic powers and protect the person wearing it.

taotie A design on Shang and Zhou Dynasty bronze vessels that combines human and animal facial features.

30

WEBSITES

Ancient China for Kids
http://china.mrdonn.org/shang&chou.html
Discover facts about the Shang and Zhou Dynasty's religion, music, warfare and more. With fun Chinese clip art.

Shang Dynasty
http://kids.britannica.com/comptons/article-9601196/ Shang-dynasty
Read *Encyclopaedia Britannica*'s informative site about the Shang.

Shang Dynasty China
http://www.historyforkids.org/learn/china/history/shang.htm
Learn all about the people, culture, inventions and religion of the Shang Dynasty.

Smithsonian Institute
http://www.pbase.com/bmcmorrow/sacklergallery&page=all
Take a close-up look at photos of amazing Shang objects on display at the Smithsonian Institute's Sackler Gallery in Washington, DC, USA.

Treasure Tomb of the Warrior Queen
http://channel.nationalgeographic.com/channel/videos/ shang-dynasty-human-sacrifice/
Watch a fascinating video about grisly human sacrifices made in Shang queen Fu Hao's tomb.

TIMELINE

1900 BCE The Xia dynasty rule in the Yellow River region of north-east China.

1600 BCE Tang overthrows the Xia leader and takes control in the Yellow River region.

1600 BCE King Tang sets up his capital city in Bo.

1600 BCE Bronze weapons, tools and religious vessels are introduced into north-east China. Warriors use chariots in battle.

1600 BCE Priests carve oracle bones with characters to ask questions of the gods. This represents China's earliest form of writing.

1600–1000 BCE Looms to weave silk cloth are introduced; Shang rulers build palaces and walled cities.

1300 BCE King Pan Geng rules. He moves the capital to Yin Xu – near modern-day Anyang.

1200 BCE King Wu Ding rules and the Shang Dynasty is at its height. His wife Fu Hao dies and is buried in a tomb filled with treasures for her use in the afterlife.

1200–1046 BCE Rulers who follow Wu Ding lose their grip on power and the dynasty begins to decline.

1046 BCE Shang slaves revolt due to cruelty and high taxes and join with the Zhou people of western China.

1046 BCE The last Shang ruler, Di Xin, is overthrown and the Zhou Dynasty begins to reign.

31

INDEX

32